# Tourney and Joust

Tourney and joust – the words conjure up a world of magic and romance. High above the arena, flags and pennants flutter bravely, while in the park below knights in glittering armour thunder down the lists to battle with each other.

The author traces the history of the tournament from its rough beginnings as a violent free-for-all to the courtly pageant of later days. He takes us behind the scenes, and describes how a big tournament was organized, with heralds issuing challenges throughout the land, and knights from far and wide arriving to defend their honour. But, above all, the book examines the tournament for what it really was, a sport, highly specialized, and with carefully defined rules, the applications of which are analyzed in detail.

The book has nearly seventy illustrations, including a set of specially commissioned drawings, which give an original and fascinating insight into the history of the tournament.



STEVEN JEFFREYS graduated in history at the University of Oxford and then spent a number of years in publishing before becoming a full-time writer. He has also written *A Medieval Siege* in the Sentinel series.

A WAYLAND SENTINEL BOOK

# Tourney and Joust

Steven Jeffreys

"When the battle begins, let men of good breeding think only of killing; nothing thrills me like the battle cry of ON! ON!, or the sight of the last dead with the pennoned stumps of lances still in their sides." (Bertrand de Borne)

## More Sentinel Books

The Story of Gunpowder *Kenneth Allen*
The Legions of Rome *Matthew Holden*
Nelson's Navy *Roger Hart*
A Medieval Siege *Steven Jeffreys*
War in the Trenches *Matthew Holden*
Genghis Khan *Michael Gibson*
The Battle of Britain *Anthony Hobbs*
The Samurai of Japan *Michael Gibson*
The French Foreign Legion *Nigel Thomas*
The Wars of the Roses *Kenneth Allen*
The Battle of the Atlantic *Kenneth Allen*

*Frontispiece* Thomas, Earl of Lancaster, Leicester, Derby and Lincoln, and Steward of England, by Colnaghi (published 1814).

ISBN 85340 185 3


49 Lansdowne Place, Hove, Sussex BN3 1HF

2nd Impression 1980

Printed by Page Bros (Norwich) Ltd., Norwich, England

# Contents

# List of Illustrations

# 1. The beginnings of a sport

It was often hard to tell the difference between a tournament (*opposite*) and an all-out battle (*above*).

In the year 1062, the French knight Godfrey of Preuilly was killed in a tournament outside the town of Tours. He was not the last man to die like this, but he is of special interest, for he was the first person to draw up a set of rules for the tournament. This remained a popular sport for the next four hundred years. As far as we know, in fact, Godfrey was the first man in the history of Europe who actually invented a sport. It was his bad luck that he should have been killed in the process.

For many years after his death, tournaments were more like all-out battles than a sport. They were fought over many square miles; hundreds of men were involved and the weapons they used were the ones designed for real warfare. It is not surprising then that many men got killed.

Like the football games of Tudor times, the tournament started as a wild, tough brawl. But, again like football, it grew in time into a great spectator sport, followed by thousands of enthusiastic fans, and with strict rules enforced by referees and officials. In this book we are going to see how the tournament, or tourney, developed over the years, and take a look at the rule-book and see how it was applied in action. We shall also discover that the tournament is being revived today by a small body of enthusiasts. It can therefore rightly claim to be Europe's oldest organized sport.

# "Fighting is fun"

For the nobleman of medieval times, warfare was a part of life; for most of them it was also the best part. From the age of seven or eight, boys were trained to manage horses and to handle the weapons of war. Soon they were charging at the quintain, a swivelling target that would knock them off their horse if they didn't hit it exactly right. This was excellent practice for the joust. Before they were fifteen, they might well be fighting in a real battle, and they expected to spend most of their life in the saddle.

Europe was full of small states struggling to be independent, and fighting each other to gain land and power. A young knight had plenty of opportunity to fight. Most of them really enjoyed it. Bertrand de Borne, who came from Provence in the South of France and is today remembered as a poet, was a typical young knight. He wrote: "I love the gay time of Easter, which brings forth the leaves and flowers, and I love the joyous song of the birds ringing through the woods. But I love too, to see the knights and horses in the meadows in battle array . . . . We are going to have a marvellous time. Trumpets and drums and horses will soon be on the field. . . . When the battle begins, let men of good breeding think only of killing. . . . nothing thrills me like the battle cry of ON! ON! or the sight of the last dead with the pennoned stumps of lances still in their sides."

The words "tourney" and "joust" are often used now as though they meant the same thing. But, strictly speaking, the joust was a combat between two men only, while many hundreds could take part in a tourney. They would be divided into two teams, each under its own leader, and at first there were very few rules indeed. The tournament was, however, supposed to last a fixed number of hours; certain types of blow, allowed in war, were banned; and both sides were

A knight tilting at the quintain, which consisted of a board pivoted on a pole, with a sandbag attached. The cross marks the point where the knight hit the target. In the top picture, he has hit it squarely, and can pass safely under the sandbag. But in the lower picture, he has missed his aim, and the sandbag has swung round to knock him off his horse.

*Left* Medieval noblemen loved a good fight. *Right* Warfare was a part of everyday life.

supposed to carry the same kind of weapons. There were also "refuges" or changing rooms, where the knights could rest, and receive first aid.

# Profits and losses

When tourneys began, there were no judges to ensure fair play – a single knight might be attacked by four or five others at once. The high ideals of chivalry were still young and success in the tourney could bring rich profits. Prisoners were taken, for example, and had to pay high ransoms or else surrender their horse and armour in order to regain their liberty. Since the profits were so high, it was a great temptation not to play fair.

Nothing was more important to a knight than his horse. He needed it in order to take part in wars and earn his living from booty and plunder. It was also a big status symbol.

Travelling could be very dangerous for a knight who had lost his horse. The knight Girart of Ruisslon had lost all his possessions in an unsuccessful campaign. As he and his wife were travelling through the countryside that he had plundered the year before, they met a company of merchants. The suspicious merchants thought they recognized the down-at-heel knight, and were ready to attack him. Girart was only saved by his wife's quick thinking, when she swore that Girart of Ruisslon was dead. "God be praised," they replied, "for he was always making war." Girart himself continues the story: "My brow darkened when I heard these words, and if I had had a sword I would have killed them there and then."

But Girart did not have his sword and, without it and his horse, a knight was scarcely a knight at all. His only hope was to find a rich lord willing to equip him for another war. A war gave knights a chance to win prisoners and hold them to ransom.

When the war was over, an ambitious knight would look around for tournaments. In one contest, a single knight took three prisoners and made himself a fortune on the proceeds. Together their ransoms produced: three warhorses; arms and armour; light horses for

Nothing was more important to a knight than a fine horse.

his servants and heavy baggage horses to carry his equipment. This would be equivalent to about £15,000 today, so it is not surprising that a successful tourneyer visited as many meetings as he could.

# Banned by kings and priests

By 1100, tournaments were taking place in most parts of northern Europe. They were to grow more and more popular as time went on and the chance of private wars grew less. Kings and central governments slowly became stronger. Kings generally preferred their subjects to fight between themselves in tournaments rather than in actual wars; even so though, they did not like the crowds of turbulent armed men who came together whenever a tournament was being held. Some kings would have liked to see tournaments stopped altogether, but this was difficult to achieve; besides, many kings enjoyed tournaments themselves.

One of the finest tournaments of the whole century was in fact held for a king. When Philip II of France was crowned in 1179, more than one thousand knights came to joust. The most important guest was Henry, the eldest son of King Henry II of England. Acres of vines were trampled down in the fighting and Prince Henry was almost captured by French knights. If kings really wanted to stop tournaments, they did not always set a very good example.

The Church objected much more strongly though and, in 1130, Pope Innocent II banned all tournaments. He was shocked that Christian knights should fight and even kill one another in the name of sport. He urged them instead to go to Palestine where he hoped they would use up their energy and love of fighting in Crusades against the Infidel. But the Crusaders themselves were soon following the European craze. They held their first tournament at Antioch (now Antakya in Turkey) in 1156 and soon there were many others.

Before the year 1200, three more popes had reissued Innocent II's ban, but it was a waste of time. Knights taking part in tournaments were sometimes excommunicated by the Church; if they were killed in the fray, their bodies might be refused burial. In a religious

Kings tried to ban tournaments, because they did not like the crowds of turbulent armed men that came together whenever a tournament was held.

age this was a very serious punishment, but it was not enough. Finally, in 1316, Pope John XXII lifted the useless bans. His excuse was that, without tournaments to train them, there would not be enough knights to go on Crusade at all!

Troubadour poets singing tales of love.

# William Marshall

Probably the most successful tourneyer of them all was the English nobleman, William Marshall. His father was a minor baron but, since William was only the fourth son, he could not expect to inherit any of the family's land. When he was thirteen, his father sent him to be a squire in the household of his cousin the Lord of Tancarville in Normandy. For eight years William served his great cousin as a squire, waiting impatiently to be dubbed a knight himself so that he could win glory in the tournament and on the battlefield.

In 1167, when he was about twenty, the great day arrived at last, and he fought heroically in his first battle. He did lose his horse, however, and had to borrow one from his lord so that he could fight in the tournament that followed soon after. This was to be held at Le Mans in France, and the knights of Anjou, Maine, Poitou and Brittany were to oppose those from England, France and Normandy. This time, William did not waste his opportunity and came back to Tancarville with a huge booty of horses and armour. Within weeks there was another tourney, and William was awarded the prize for the finest performance.

The turning point in William's life, however, really came the next year – strangely enough because he had been taken prisoner. He had been captured in a battle to defend Queen Eleanor, wife of Henry II, King of England, and in her own right the ruler of the great duchy of Aquitaine in southern France. Eleanor was one of the most beautiful women of her day and also one of the most powerful. Her lands were the home of the troubadour poets who, in their songs and ballads, were spreading a new ideal of love and courtly chivalry. She was their patroness, and her court became a centre for their new way of life.

Queen Eleanor had been so impressed by William's bravery that she helped him arrange his ransom and so

Queen Eleanor of Aquitaine, who was very impressed by William Marshall's bravery, and helped to arrange his release from captivity.

got him released. To win the approval of Queen Eleanor was perhaps the most important thing a young knight could do, next to earning a reputation in the tournament. Before he was twenty-two, William Marshall had done both.

## From tourneyer to senior statesman

Next year, his reputation as a tourneyer and his friendship with the royal house of England brought William a still greater honour. King Henry II appointed him to be the sole tutor of his eldest son and heir, Prince Henry, for everything to do with chivalry. It was William Marshall, once only a landless knight, who admitted the Prince into the order of knighthood when the time came.

Later the Prince took his retainers to France where they plunged into the round of tourneys and feasts kept up by the French nobility. It was William's job to act as bodyguard for his master and make sure that the heir to the crown of England was not killed or held to ransom. It was a pretty hard job too, because in those days nobody would have hesitated to take a man prisoner just because he was a king's son.

Prince Henry died in 1183 and, on his deathbed, he made William promise that he would go on a Crusade to the Holy Land. When he returned four years later, William was admitted into the household of King Henry II who admired him for his loyalty to the prince and gave him lands. From now on, William spent all his time in politics or else looking after his estates. He left the tournament to others.

William Marshall won both fame and riches through being a champion jouster. But he was one of the last to do so. For, although the tournament meant big profits for the winners, losing many times could make even a very rich man really poor. Soon rich and noble families were unwilling to risk so much wealth and social status in the rough and tumble of the tournament and began to insist on stronger rules. By the time William Marshall retired from the sport it was already becoming highly organized.

A sixteenth-century German woodcut, showing a medieval knight setting out proudly on Crusade to the Holy Land.

## 2. The legends of King Arthur

The tournament gradually became part of a new code of chivalry growing up in Europe in the eleventh and twelfth centuries. The order of knighthood was the most honourable that any nobleman, whether king or lowly baron, could belong to, and only knights could take part in tournaments.

In the eleventh century, churchmen were persuading knights to bring religion into their ceremonies. A man was admitted to knighthood by being "dubbed" with a sword tap on his shoulder, and by having his sword belt tied up round his waist by another knight. Now this began to be done in church, and the young would-be knight would spend a whole night praying alone before the altar.

So, when the tournament really got under way, knights were beginning to think of themselves as God's soldiers, with special rights and special duties. They were very proud of their order, although their actions did not often live up to their high claims. When the Crusades began in 1096, the business of fighting became even more honourable. Soon the idea of the Christian knight became the centre of an entirely new way of life and a code for social behaviour. It even had its own legends and poems.

These were the stories of King Arthur. They told of an ancient king of Britain who, with his band of knights, defended his country from invading heathens, travelling around to defeat monsters and protect the weak. It was these romantic stories that shaped the chivalric world of the tournament for centuries to come.

The Vigil – a young would-be knight praying alone before the altar.

# Bards and scholars

Even today, people who live in the British Isles tend to think of King Arthur as their especial property. After all the stories describe him as a British king. But in fact, during the Middle Ages, the stories were known and loved all over Europe.

The stories seem to have started in Wales. As the Normans pushed their conquest into the valleys of South Wales, they took with them story-tellers and poets. Many of these were men from Brittany, who had come with their lords across the English Channel in the army of William the Conqueror in 1066. Bretons and Welshmen are both of Celtic ancestry and even today can understand one another's languages. These ancient bards thrilled to the marvellous tales they heard from the courts of the Welsh princes.

When they returned to their own country these Breton poets, or *fabulatores* as they are called in the chronicles, spread the stories far and wide. At least one Welsh bard, called Bleheris, also travelled to Europe with the songs of his people and won great fame at the court of Count William of Poitou.

All these stories were known to people in Europe as "the matter of Britain." They were collected at the beginning of the twelfth century in an extraordinary book called *The History of the Kings of Britain,* by Geoffrey of Monmouth. He was a scholar, probably a Welshman, who lived in Oxford but claimed that all his material came from old Welsh sources. Only forty years after Geoffrey's death, a chronicler accused him of inventing the whole thing. The chronicler may well have been right, but by then it was too late.

Geoffrey's book, and still more romantic versions written by other men, had spread everywhere. The legend of King Arthur and his Round Table, the names of the heroes Sir Gawain, Sir Lancelot, Sir Galahad and Sir Kay, the story of Queen Guinevere and many

Medieval bards, who spread the stories of King Arthur and his knights.

others were eagerly read and talked about in courts and castles all over Europe. The tales of knights "errant" (the old French for "wandering"), travelling the world in quest of adventure, inspired many young noblemen.

# Knights in love

The stories of King Arthur and his companions gave knights an honourable picture of themselves as soldiers. At the same time, the troubadours of Provence had been describing in their poetry a new kind of love. They talked of women as beautiful and mysterious creatures who had great power over their lovers; men who hoped to win their favours had to be humble and obedient. Soon rough warriors who had been used to telling their women what to do were caught up in the fashion and heaved sad sighs of passion – when they remembered to.

All these romantic ideas began to change the idea of the tournament. A totally new kind of tournament evolved, called a "Round Table"; this began with the competitors taking strict vows to behave honourably and to obey the laws of chivalry, as King Arthur and his companions were thought to have done. Ladies were given the seats of honour in the stands to watch the noble proceedings. The men taking part sometimes dressed themselves up in costumes representing the Arthurian heroes. Some turned up anonymously as "knights errant" and the fighting became just one part of a great festival of chivalry, which included side shows, and all sorts of sporting contests apart from the joust itself. The first Round Table we know about took place in 1223, on the island of Cyprus in the Mediterranean. In England, a Round Table was the occasion for all sorts of sporting contests, including "casting the stone" (the ancestor of the shot putt) and lance throwing.

A few years later, a German knight called Ulrich of Lichtenstein had a still more fantastic idea. He travelled around parts of Austria, Italy and Bohemia saying that he would defend the honour of his lady against all comers. If Ulrich won, the other knight would have to

*Opposite* Knights fought to win the favour of their ladies, who were given seats of honour in the stands.

*Below* A lovesick knight.

bow to the four corners of the earth in her honour. If Ulrich lost, he promised to give the winner a prize of horses. Ulrich had a special costume made to represent Venus, the goddess of love and wore this for some of the challenges; the tour was a great success.

Later on Ulrich made another jousting tour dressed this time as King Arthur. After him many others played at being knight errants.

# A royal enthusiast

Obviously the tournaments were becoming much more refined than before, but fighting and brawling could still break out from time to time. In 1267, many years after Ulrich had been charming people with his gentlemanly games, King Edward I of England passed a Statute of Arms in order to stop the rioting that went on at tournaments. It gives us a frightening picture of what things must have been like before. For example, the King ordered that spectators were not allowed to be

This is the sort of rioting that Edward I hoped to stop when he passed his Statute of Arms in 1267.

armed and, among the officials, only squires and heralds were to carry weapons; the standard bearers could only have protective armour. If anyone was found carrying a weapon without permission, he could be sent to prison. Finally the King ordered that anyone coming into the enclosure had to wear the badge or colours of one of the competitors.

King Edward also at times banned tourneying completely. He wanted to stop his barons from wasting their energies on sport when he needed them for his wars against the Welsh and the Scots. But when a campaign was over the King would often hold a tournament himself so as to be popular with his nobles and make them all feel part of a loyal national effort.

Edward was a real Arthurian enthusiast. His own marriage in 1299 was marked by another tournament and "according to the custom, a play of King Arthur was enacted." Some of the parts were played by young squires dressed up as characters from the Arthurian legends and at intervals in the show other squires rode in to call on the company to take up arms against the Scots. For Edward realized that his knights were so attached to the ideals of chivalry that a tournament could be a very good opportunity to encourage them to fight on his behalf.

Edward had also been a keen tourneyer when he was young, although his first tour in France had not been very successful. He was beaten two or three times and lost both horses and armour. Once, even after he became king, he jousted with an enemy baron during a lull in a battle. This time he was winning, but then his enemy tried to pull him off his horse. That was against the rules and Edward's supporters piled in, killing many of the opposition.

# Infantry on the battlefield

As long as battles were only won by cavalry, the joust was good training for war as well as being fun.

But then, during the fourteenth century, warfare began to change. Foot soldiers began to win battles against horsemen. In Switzerland, citizens and peasants banded together against their rulers, and discovered a way of fighting with long pikes that made it almost impossible for the cavalry to defeat them. In the Netherlands (modern Belgium and Holland), citizen armies were using the same kind of tactics against the French king and their own dukes and counts. The most famous victories of foot soldiers over horsemen were won by the English archers against French knights at Crécy (1346) and Poitiers (1356).

All this meant that the mounted knight was no longer the most important man on the battlefield. And so his mock battles in the tournament park became even more full of pageantry since he was of less practical value as a fighting man. The one advantage of the heavy feudal cavalry had been the force of its charge; once commanders began to find answers to this, cavalry lost much of its influence.

The Swiss infantry, for example, fought with pikes and halberds. These rather crude weapons could be up to twelve feet long and made it possible for the pikemen to put up a sort of advance barrier and break the cavalry charge even before it had reached their line. The English at Crécy used archers to the same purpose. The charging horses were mown down at a distance. The superbly-armed knights of France fell to the ground before they had even had a chance to grapple with the English. These methods were not perhaps very chivalrous, but they were very effective.

In time, knights got used to being ordered to dismount from their horses and go into battle on foot. When they were marching in a solid mass, they stood a much better chance against the archers or the pikemen because of

The Battle of Poitiers
*Opposite* English archers defeat the French cavalry. *Above* The French horsemen have to dismount in order to fight on equal terms.

their greater weight. Perhaps it is not surprising that at about this time fighting on foot became a standard part of the tournament.

# The Order of the Garter

The battles of Crécy and Poitiers were won by the armies of Edward III (1312–77), one of England's greatest kings. It was also Edward who founded the first Order of chivalry. This was the Order of the Garter,

Edward III picks up the Countess of Salisbury's garter. This led later to the founding of the Order of the Garter.

which held its first meeting on St. George's Day, 1349, and has since had an honoured and unbroken history – knights of the Garter are still appointed today. The idea for the Order took shape in the King's mind at a Round Table tournament held at Windsor Castle in January 1344; he had originally meant it to be an Order of the Round Table. The Order of the Garter as we know it today started life firmly in the world of the tourney and the joust.

Historians used to think that the traditional story of the founding of the Order was just a happy legend; modern research, however, suggests that there is much truth in it. The story tells how, during a feast at Calais, in August 1347, the King was dancing with the young Countess of Salisbury, when one of her stocking garters slipped off her leg to the floor. Seeing that she was very embarrassed, the King stooped down, picked up the garter and bound it on his own leg. When some of the courtiers joked about what had happened, King Edward silenced them with these angry words: "Shame on anyone who thinks that there is anything to be ashamed of." The French words the King actually used are still the motto of the Order: "Honi soit qui mal y pense."

The Order soon became what it has since remained, the most renowned and honourable order of chivalry in Europe. One reason for its renown was that it was very small. Including the sovereign, there were only twenty-six members at any one time – a very select group. The members were forbidden to take up arms against one another. The King thus made clever use of the ideals of chivalry and the tournament. He saw that men who were bound together in a solemn vow would be unlikely to fight one another or, more important, to rebel against the sovereign of their Order.

# A new approach

Later on, English kings sometimes made foreign monarchs members of the Order of the Garter, hoping that they might then feel honour-bound not to attack England. And at least one ruler, Philip the Good, Duke of Burgundy, refused to join the Order just so that he would not be committed to an alliance with England that he might later regret. The same Philip the Good also founded an Order of chivalry in imitation of the Order of the Garter. This was the Order of the Golden Fleece.

These orders of chivalry coincided with a new phase in the history of the tourney and joust. Tournaments became more and more elaborate, and real warfare was taken over by professionals. All over Europe, rulers were hiring mercenaries since they felt that their wars would be better fought by hired soldiers than by men who were only fighting out of a sense of forced duty. The old virtues of honour and chivalry became more confined to the mock battle of the tourney, and less a part of the real battlefield. The noblemen began to make a game out of things that had once been at the centre of their lives.

Of course they still took the game very seriously. When we come to look at the importance of the tournament at the Court of Burgundy in the next century, we shall see just how serious they were. But the tournament had less and less to do with war and more and more to do with sport and entertainment.

Sometimes the jousting was held in town squares, watched by the common citizens. At other times, plays and pageants and dancing took up more time than the actual fighting. Men fought not only for their sense of personal pride, but to win the favours of their ladies. At first, any knight had had the right to enter a tournament; now, however, some writers and experts began to claim that men below a certain income

The tournament became more and more elaborate, as knights tried to attract the favourable attention of their ladies.

bracket should be excluded. In fact, the sport soon became so expensive so that many men simply could not take part. That did not make it less interesting but it did make it more select.

# 3. Tournament and joust

The tournament was certainly a spectacular entertainment, with colourful displays and legendary heroes. For those taking part however, it also meant a lot of training, a lot of hard work and, if you wanted to hold your own tournament, a lot of money. Like any sport, it was a way of life for its enthusiasts. Men became knights errant, and spent most of their time just going from one joust to another. Some men took the whole business so seriously that they spent all their fortune on it, and were left destitute.

Others wrote long and learned books on the sport; about how to hold a tournament, for example, or how to issue challenges. There was *The Book of Chivalry and Knighthood*, by the Spanish nobleman Ramon Lull, and *The Book of the Tourney* by Duke René of Anjou. In the middle of the fifteenth century, an anonymous French author even claimed to tell *How they held Tournaments and Assemblies at the Court of Utherpendragon and of King Arthur*. It does not matter that King Arthur did not hold tournaments at all. The author was pretending to write history, but he was really doing something quite different. He was describing how *he* thought anyone who wanted to give a really good tournament should set about it.

*Right* A scribe copying out a learned book about the tournament.

*Left* A knight errant, travelling from joust to joust.

# How to hold a tournament

Kings and princes usually arranged tournaments for special state occasions, or else for propaganda purposes. Wealthy aristocrats on the other hand might hold one just for pleasure, much as a rich man today would throw a big party. One of the great events of the fifteenth century was the *pas d'armes*, or passage of arms, given by Pierre Bauffrement Lord of Charny, in 1443. The party lasted for two months and spread into three great castles which the Lord of Charny had opened for his hundreds of guests.

In one of the castles, the competitors prepared for the combat, and each one was given his own room in which to keep his armour and weapons. In a second castle, the guests could find light snacks and wine at any time of the day. The third castle was reserved for the splendid feasts and banquets that were held two or three times a week.

A passage of arms was just a tournament with a particularly dramatic setting. The people holding the tournament pretended that they were knights of old defending a mountain pass. Anyone who wanted to get through had to defeat one of them in a personal joust. It gave everyone a chance to dress-up and relive the glorious ideals of King Arthur and the Round Table.

Lord Charny called his *pas d'armes* "The Tree of Charlemagne", in honour of the great hero of French legend, Roland, who had saved the armies of the Emperor Charlemagne by holding a pass in the Pyrenees against the Moors. There were to be forty days of fighting, and the competition and entertainments spread over two months starting on 1st July.

*Opposite* Preparations for a tournament.

In March, Lord Charny sent heralds to carry his challenge to all princes, barons, knights and squires "without a stain on their honour." He assured competitors that he and his twelve friends who were defending the pass were all knights from old families,

and were not holding the tournament to make a reputation for themselves, but purely "to exalt the noble profession of arms."

# The Tree of Charlemagne

The challenge was issued in the name of St. George, who was one of the patron saints of the order of knight-

*Left* The Tree of Charlemagne, with the two challenge shields set up on either side.

hood. It started with careful directions on how to find the "pass", which was marked by the Tree of Charlemagne. The tree was draped with the coat of arms of the Charny family and on either side were two shields. On the right side was a violet shield decorated with black tears; on the left a black one, decorated with golden tears. Anyone who wanted to joust touched the black shield; anyone wanting to fight on foot touched the violet shield.

The contestants were expected from Spain, England, Germany and Italy. Of course, they would all pretend to be knights errant wandering up hill and down dale and arriving just by chance at the Tree of Charlemagne on 1st July; but since there would be absolute chaos if they all turned up out of the blue, the officials wanted a definite list of names and a programme settled before the passage of arms began.

Next, the challenge laid down the rules under which the fights were to be held, and the kind of weapons and armour to be used. The chief prizes were also described – for example, anyone who defeated one of the champions defending the pass would receive a ransom of five hundred golden crowns. This was an enormous sum, and was meant to show how proud and noble the defenders were. But they were careful too. It would be possible for a really strong and expert visitor to win himself a fortune and bankrupt the defenders by challenging the weakest of them again and again. So the rules laid down that each visitor could ask for only one combat with each of the defenders of the pass.

More than fifty contestants entered and they were all attended by squires and servants; many other noblemen and great ladies came as spectators. The cost of just feeding all these people for week after week was phenomenal; and there were in addition the prizes to be paid for, and weapons provided for those who did not have the right kind. You certainly had to be rich to put on a tournament like this.

Heralds issuing the challenge, as a knight rides forth.

# Challenges of chivalry

A man who enjoyed jousting, but could not afford to hold a tournament, would set out as a knight errant. Very often, he would bind some token or "gauge" to his leg, as the symbol of his love for his lady.

In May 1400, for example, Sir Michael d'Orris, a knight of the Spanish kingdom of Aragon, issued an open challenge to the chivalry of England. It started: "In the name of God. Be it known that I, wishing to exalt my reputation and knowing the fame of the English chivalry have attached this day to my leg a piece of armour that shall stay there until I am delivered of it by an English knight performing the following feats of arms." He then listed various kinds of combat. However, when an English knight, Sir John Prendergast, offered to take up the challenge, the Spaniard all of a sudden became rather difficult to find.

But what usually happened in cases like this was that the challenger went up to the knight errant, solemnly touched the gauge and demanded a joust. If they had fought well, the knight errant then felt he could take off the gauge.

On another occasion a French knight came to England and travelled up and down the kingdom issuing challenge after challenge. But nobody came forward. It was during a time when the King of England had banned all jousting and tournaments. The Frenchmen went back to Dover with a rather low opinion of English chivalry.

But news of his challenge reached a Welsh knight, who felt very ashamed that a foreigner could come to Britain looking for adventure and not find it. He rode hard to Dover and just missed the Frenchman's ship. So he hired a fishing boat, caught up with the French knight, and, there and then, on board ship in the middle of the English Channel, he touched the gauge on his leg and sailed on with him to joust in France.

*Below* A Welsh knight takes up the Frenchman's challenge by touching the gauge on his leg.

*Above* A knight being handed his helmet by his lady before setting out on his travels.

# Weapons and armour

Touching a lady's handkerchief tied to a knight's leg may seem a strange way to win the right for a duel of honour. But the fight itself was real enough. Knights were part-time soldiers, and men were sometimes killed in the joust. So one of the most important things to be settled before a joust was the kind of weapons that were to be used.

Normally the weapons used in the joust were rebated, or treated in some way to make them less dangerous. The sword edges were blunted and the points were rounded, while the ends of the lances were splayed out and then bound up again so as to give a wide stubby end called a "coronal". Sometimes, however, a tournament was fought with weapons *à outrance* meaning "to the bitter end", and then they were sharp and pointed and very dangerous.

The rules for a tournament were fairly detailed on the subject of weapons, but they did not often have much to say about armour. Usually a man was free to choose his own armour, and most people would probably be wearing whatever was fashionable at the time.

In the days of William Marshall, armour had consisted basically of chain mail – thousands of interlinking iron rings hammered together. By the fifteenth century, a suit of armour was made of solid steel plates, and a good armourer had to be as skilled as a tailor to fit the suit. Armour was very heavy, and sometimes weighed nearly as much as the man himself. A skilled craftsman could shape the plates so perfectly that they fitted every curve of the body; the armour then moved easily with the body, and seemed much lighter than it really was. The best armourers were in Milan in Italy and Nuremberg in Germany. Before a great joust, even English noblemen would go to Milan to order their armour. Many of these suits survive and they are really beautiful works of art.

*Below* A suit of German armour.

*Above* A knight removing his coat of chain mail.

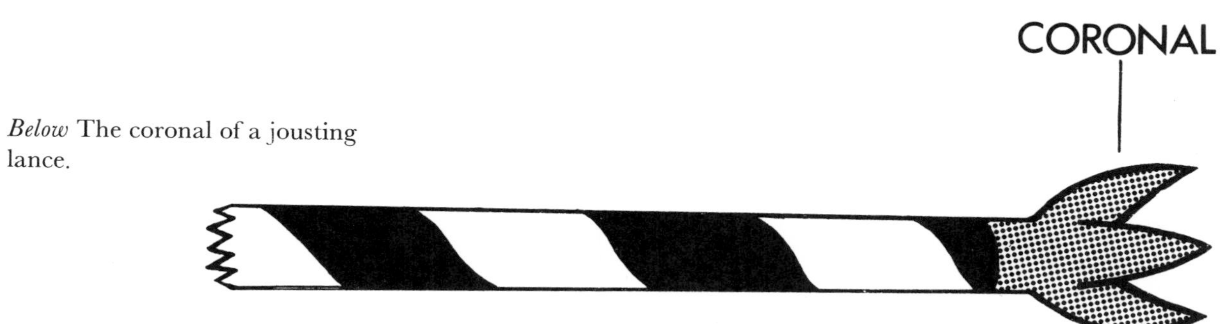


*Below* The coronal of a jousting lance.

## Refinements in armour

To improve their armour, the designers curved the plates in various ways so that the enemy lance would slip away. Then they piled more and more pieces of defensive equipment onto one suit. In the end, the knights could hardly move in their iron cages and the horses could scarcely carry their fantastic weight – the joust slowed down to a jog trot.

Helmets developed too. One of the first improvements was a hinged face guard or "vizor", which could be pulled down in battle, or else pushed back to let the wearer get a breath of air without having to take off his whole helmet. But it proved impossible to make a helmet which would give a clear and easy view and, at the same time, protect the face completely. So the helmet was probably the weakest part of the whole magnificent jouster's outfit.

His horse was the single most valuable thing a jouster had to buy and it cost a great deal. There were many different kinds of horses, but the best of them all was the "destrier", tremendously strong but fast as well. Of our modern breeds, the percheron is probably most like the magnificent destriers of the Middle Ages. With a huge man like King Henry VIII, wearing his great suit of jousting armour, the horse would have about thirty stone on his back before he started. And then he had to charge at full speed down the lists. In battle, destriers were trained to rear up on their hind legs and batter the enemy with their front hooves.

A keen tourneyer would need to have two or three of these superb beasts in his stable to use as remounts. Then he would want a good "sumpter" or baggage horse to carry all his equipment; "palfreys" for his squires; and horses of some kind, even if only second-rate "rounceys", for his servants. Of these, only the destrier had to be a thoroughbred, but men would buy their mounts from distant parts to be sure of good ones.

Two knights jousting. Note the vizors on their helmets.

*Below* Armour became so heavy that knights had to be lifted up by a system of pulleys onto their horses.

# Pageant and heraldry

*Above* An artist's impression of the royal coat of arms.

Each competitor arrived at the tournament with a cavalcade of squires and servants at his back, all dressed in "livery" decorated with his coat of arms. From the stands, banners and flags fluttered gaily, displaying the crests of the men holding the tournament, while the contestants in the arena proudly wore their own coats of arms.

The designs on these crests were not just beautiful, they meant a great deal. The right to wear a personal coat of arms was a privilege of nobility, and you were only allowed to use a design if it had been duly registered at the Royal College of Heralds. Some experts thought that a man should not be allowed to take part in a tournament if his family's coat of arms had not been registered for at least seventy years.

From time to time, the heralds toured around the country and checked up on everybody who was using a "device". If they were doing so without permission, they could be fined very heavily and if, through some mistake, they were using the same design as another family, a lawsuit was bound to follow. There was a special Court of Chivalry to try such cases.

The most famous dispute in fourteenth-century England was fought between the families of Scrope and Grosvenor, to decide who had the right to use the design of a blue shield with a wide diagonal gold band across it. The dispute went on for many years, and aroused much bitterness. In a world where honour counted for almost everything, and where the coat of arms symbolized a family's honour, it is easy to see why the case should have been so important.

Such disputes would have been much more frequent had there not been any record of existing devices. In fact the College of Heralds kept a "roll of arms", and they also developed a special technical language for describing all the hundreds of different shield designs.

*Opposite* A knight in full livery.

# The language of heraldry

The first thing a herald would describe about a shield was its background colour or "field"; he would then list all the shapes or "charges" on it in a special order. The Old French language of the medieval heralds is still used today by the English College of Heralds. A simple design like the Scrope/Grosvenor arms was easy to describe. It was: *azure* (blue), to describe the background field, *a bend or* ("*bend*" is the heraldic term for a wide diagonal band, and "*or*" means gold). However complicated the design, the language of the heralds

*Opposite* The distinctive heraldic emblems made it possible to recognize contestants at a glance.

could describe it so precisely that it could never be confused with any other.

Every ruler and many great aristocrats had their own "king-at-arms" whose duty it was to make all the arrangements for a big tournament. In the arena itself, the heraldic emblems and the crests on the helmets made it possible to recognize the contestants even when they were covered from head to toe with armour. The emblems were not only carried on the shield but also on the surcoat over the armour and on the mantling that covered the horses' armour. Experts in the crowd could easily read even a stranger's coat of arms. For example, it would tell them what families he was related to, or whether he had any royal blood in his veins, whether he was the eldest son or not, what country he came from, and many other things. For this reason, when a knight decided to travel anonymously, he left his crest and coat of arms at home.

The colourful coats of arms were very useful to the king-at-arms as he booked foreign knights into the competition. No-one would dare to wear arms that he was not entitled to, and the officials could see immediately whether a competitor should be allowed into the lists or not. Before a great tournament opened, the knights were expected to put their crests and coats of arms on display for a final check by the officials. If they discovered even at this late stage that one of the contestants had a dishonourable incident in his past, they solemnly disqualified him, and his helmet was shamefully thrown out of the display.

This did not happen very often.

*Below* Heralds making a tour of inspection before a big tournament, to check that all the arms are in order.

# 4 The rules of the game

The judge presiding at a joust.

A big tournament was a very colourful occasion, but it was also a sport and needed to have rules and regulations. In this chapter we shall take a look at the rule book, and see what kind of problems the referee, or judge, had to deal with. As we shall see, he sometimes had to make very tricky decisions.

Of course, if there are rules, someone will always try to break them whatever the game. There was cheating in the tournament, just as there are fouls in football, But, perhaps because everyone was thinking of his honour, cheating was not all that frequent.

Behind all the magnificent display, there were twenty or thirty young men fighting for the applause of the crowd and a kiss or a smile from their sweethearts. Most of them "did the circuit", going from joust to joust and trying to work their way up the unofficial table of champions. Anyone who was interested in the game knew how each of the regulars was rated. There was a system of scoring too, and some of the old scoring cards still survive.

A tournament attracted huge crowds, local villagers and craftsmen, tenants watching their lords. They thrilled to the excitement of the battles, the glamour of the trappings and the fanfares of the heralds; but many of them could also follow the finer points of the play.

# Scoring a bout

Jousting shields were curved to deflect blows.

The simplest form of tournament scoring gave victory to the man who shattered the most lances. The contest had a set number of rounds or "courses", in which each knight charged once; in this type of joust, unhorsing your opponent was a valuable bonus, but the main object was to break your lance on his shield.

This was not always as easy as it might sound. The lances were about twelve feet long and keeping the point on target as your horse charged, and perhaps even bucked underneath you, called for great skill. Another problem was the shield itself. It was usually quite small and hard to hit, and was often curved in order to throw off the point of the lance before it had a chance to lodge and shatter.

In later years, the scoring became more complicated. About 1465, John Tiptoft, the Earl of Worcester, drew up a scoring system for English tournaments, in which the highest points were awarded for unhorsing your opponent. Other good scoring hits were a blow to the crest on the enemy's helmet, or else breaking the largest number of lances. The knight who stayed the longest time in the lists, and was reckoned to have kept up the highest average standard of play, won additional bonus points.

One of the most difficult manoeuvres of all was to catch the coronal (or point) of your enemy's lance with your own, since both horsemen had to have very steady hands to do it. Points were lost for hitting the barrier, or the saddle of the oncoming horse.

The joust, with points counted up to decide the winner, was very different from the tournament of the old days, when there was not even a barrier to divide the opponents. Before the start of big contests, the heralds made the "customary cries in the four corners of the lists" that no one was to help the contestants even by shouting words of advice. Squires were allowed

*Above* A blow to the crest on your enemy's helmet was a good scoring hit.
*Below* A squire holding his master's sword by the point.

into the arena to hand new weapons to their masters, but they had to hold the swords by their points so that they would not be tempted to join in the fight.

*Below* The best way to score in jousting was to break your lance on your enemy's shield, as the two knights in the picture have done.

There were foot battles in the tournament as well.

## Rules and regulations

Arranging a big joust was a serious business and needed a lot of planning. Once the knights had assembled, the rules of the contest had to be announced. They included: the number of courses to be run in the mounted events; the height of the barrier, usually about six feet; and the penalty to be paid to his opponent by someone unhorsed by "direct blow with the lance". There were regulations for the foot battles as well. The winner here was usually the one who did the most damage in a set number of blows. There were special penalties against the knight who fell to his knees or who had to

*Above* There were special penalties for a knight who fell to his knees.

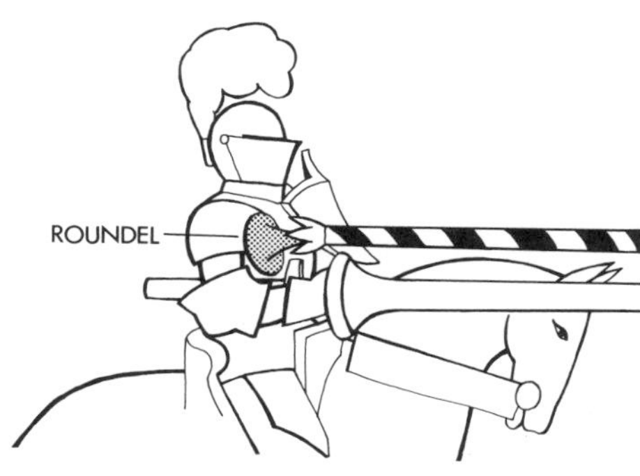


*Above* A clever opponent could catch the coronal of his lance on the roundel, and keep himself out of reach.

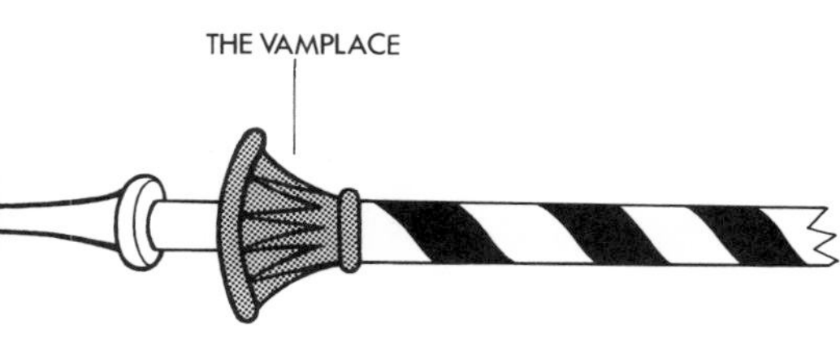


*Above* A vamplace, or hand guard, on a jousting lance.

steady himself with a hand on the ground. A full fall lost you the contest whether the set number of blows had been exchanged or not – just as a knock-out ends a modern boxing match whatever round it happens to be in.

An important regulation concerned the type of armour and weapons to be used. In most cases, the knights were free to choose their own armour as long as it was free from any additions. Some additions were very useful in war, but were a disadvantage to the jouster. These were the "roundels" which were strapped over the joints of a suit of armour to deflect sword blows. In battle they were essential, but in the joust they could lose you points. A clever opponent who could catch them with the coronal of his lance could keep himself out of your reach – even though you might both be using weapons that had been carefully measured to a certain size.

Of course there were standard sizes of weapons, but sometimes the organizer of a joust, or "*entrepreneur*", announced definite specifications. The Lord of Charny, for example, not only stated the length of the lances to be used in his *pas d'armes*, but also the width of the "vamplace" or hand guard, which was not to be more than four fingers wide. Anyone whose weapons did not meet the specifications could borrow a set for the contest.

# The officials

With all these rules and regulations, there obviously had to be someone to enforce them. Usually there were one or two judges sitting in the grandstand and a number of other officials in the arena. The officials out on the pitch were also there to separate the contestants if they lost their tempers and began to fight in earnest. It was their job, too, to help unhorsed men clamber to their feet.

The judge had the final say, but it was not always easy to make proud noblemen accept his decision. So it was obviously essential that the umpire should have a high noble rank as well as being an expert in the rules of the tournament. There might even be two judges. On one occasion the marshal of Burgundy presided at a tournament as technical expert, and the ten-year-old Crown Prince was also a judge. The young Prince couldn't decide all the technical points himself but, as the son of the Duke, he was the second most important man in Burgundy, and everybody was bound to accept his decisions.

The judge signalled the start of the proceedings by waving a short white baton; if he decided a fight had to be stopped, he threw the baton down into the ring. In the later days of the tournament a fight could be stopped if a man had obviously been very seriously wounded. Once the judge had made his decision, it had to be obeyed, and the officials in the ring had to enforce it if necessary. They wore armour of course, but instead of weapons they carried long white staves with which to separate the contestants. Usually there were between four and eight officials like this; but sometimes, even when the meeting was well organized, the judge might expect trouble and increase the number of stewards in the ring.

*Opposite* Two judges and some officials preside at a tilting match.

# "Foul play!"

When William Marshall jousted, there had been no officials or umpires at all. Nor had the rules been as strict. But the chance of riches that the tournament offered to a poor knight were a big temptation to use unfair tactics or outright foul play. Even a great nobleman might bend the rules more than somewhat.

Count Philip of Flanders, for example, was called the "Flower of Chivalry" by his courtiers, but not everybody shared their flattering opinion. In fact Count Philip was greedy and wanted to make money out of the tournament just as much as any poor knight. He used to hold his men back until all the other knights

The chance the tournament offered to make a lot of money caused many knights to use unfair tactics.

had tired themselves out in the tournament with hours of fighting; then, just before it all broke up, he would ride in and take as many prisoners as possible. It was not actually against the rules, since these scarcely existed. But it was not the way people expected the "Flower of Chivalry" to behave either.

William Marshall himself found the answer. On his advice, his master Prince Henry announced that he would not be taking part in the next tournament. As usual Count Philip waited on the side lines almost till the end, before going into the attack. He was very surprised indeed when Prince Henry and his men turned up after all, later still, and this time took the count and his team prisoners.

By the fifteenth century however, tricks like this had become more difficult, and men quickly lost their tempers when they thought someone was cheating. There was a nasty argument, for example, when Lord Wells was thrown from his horse. He was so furious that he accused his opponent of having his armour screwed onto his horse's saddle before strapping himself into it. This was a dreadful insult, and Lord Wells had to apologize when the judge proved him wrong.

But sometimes there was cheating in earnest. One of the simplest tricks was to have a special gauntlet that would lock onto the grip of one's lance, and help to keep it steady. This was a great advantage, but the penalty for being found out was disqualification.

Before entering a tournament, the contestants had to swear to abide by the rules of chivalry.

*Above* Great spikes were hidden under the mantling of the Castilian's horse.

# More dirty tricks

There was a serious case of foul play at the tournament of Charlemagne's Tree in 1443. The jousts were being run without a barrier between the horses so that the riders were expected to crash into one another occasionally. The man with the heavier horse would obviously come off best and could use his greater weight to advantage. But Galiot de Baltasar, a Castilian knight, went one better. He got an armourer to fix long spikes onto his horse's armour so that he could ram the horse of his opponent, the Lord of Ternant, really viciously. At the start of the fight the spikes were hidden under the magnificent draperies that covered the horse; but when Ternant complained to the judge, the Castilian's horse was examined and he was ordered to remove the spikes. His claim that such additions were allowed in Spain saved him from being disqualified, but not everyone believed him.

A few years later in England, it seemed as if the same trick was being played. The contestants were Anthony, called the Bastard of Burgundy, and Lord Scales. In one charge, the two horses collided heavily and Lord Anthony's horse was killed outright when its head crashed into his opponent's saddle. Immediately King Edward IV, who was presiding, left the president's box to inspect the saddle himself. But there was no evidence of foul play and the contest continued.

Examples like these show that even in the fifteenth century, fouls could happen occasionally, but they were fairly unusual. The game had become so expensive that only the very rich could afford to enter for it. Even though the prizes were magnificent, nobody would have dreamt of entering the lists just to win a prize; they did not need the money that desperately. The great thing was to win fame by doing great and honourable deeds. To win by cheating was far worse than to lose honourably.

# Some difficult decisions

The judge did not often have to settle appeals against foul play, but he did have to make difficult decisions as to whether or not a particular rule had been broken. His decisions would be hotly discussed by the experts in the stands.

For example, during a joust between the Burgundian Lord Lalain, one of the most famous jousters of all time, and Boniface, a knight from Aragon, Lalain's lance, obviously a faulty one, had split right down the middle, from the tip up to the hand guard. But it had not shattered in the technical sense of the word and the knight from Aragon claimed that his enemy must continue to fight with it until it did. Lalain accepted this, since he thought it would be dishonourable to bend the rules in his own favour. But his supporters protested strongly and the situation looked impossible.

Strictly speaking, the knight from Aragon was right, but if the fight were to go on, Lalain had no hope with his lance flopping uselessly about. The judge was completely perplexed, and the experts were shouting all sorts of contradictory advice. A quick-witted official found the answer. He took the split lance and forced his baton down it like a wedge so that the two halves splayed apart. Then he went across to Boniface and, in a voice that everyone could hear, asked him if, as a man of honour, he could really fight an enemy at such a disadvantage. Boniface was thus forced to let his opponent take a new lance.

In another fight, a sword fight between the Lord of Ternant and Galiot the Castilian, Ternant's sword jammed in the scabbard. When he finally wrenched it free, it slipped out of his hand and got stuck in his horse's harness, just out of reach. He then had to try and defend himself just with his arm and mailed fist, while Galiot hit him again and again with his sword. The judge could only stop the fight when Ternant's

*Below left* The official forced his baton down the split lance. *Centre* The sword got stuck in the horse's harness, just out of reach. *Right* So as not to lose their weapons, many knights attached them to their armour with cords.

sword dropped to the ground and he was, at last, technically unarmed.

So as not to lose their weapons in this way, many knights had them attached by cords to their armour.

# A question of honour

*Opposite* Tournament fights were often very dangerous.

Often the rules were not absolutely clear, and there was no international board of control like there is for most sports today. Judges often made decisions which clearly favoured the home player.

At the Tourney of the Fair Pilgrim, for example, the judge was Duke Philip of Burgundy, and the contestants came from all over Europe. One of them, a Spanish knight called Bernard of Bearne, was jousting with the Lord of Halbourdin when his helmet was lifted off by his enemy's lance. Bernard's squire had not bolted it on properly. Halbourdin got in three hard blows to the face before Duke Philip stopped the fight. The Duke seemed to be helping the Spaniard; but Bernard burst into tears and begged the Duke to let the fight continue! He said he had travelled hundreds of miles to win honour for himself at this tourney and unless he was given the chance to beat the Frenchman even without his helmet, his reputation would be ruined. The Duke stuck to his decision, but he promised the brave young knight that no-one thought any the worse of him. A man did not have to be killed to prove his bravery.

However, when the honour of a Burgundian knight was at stake in a similar way, Duke Philip took rather a different view. Later on at the same tourney, the renowned Jacques Lalain was fighting with the Welsh knight Sir Thomas Key. The Welshman had got the upper hand and many spectators thought that Lalain was signalling the Duke to stop the fight. He was bleeding heavily from his left arm and was in a very bad way. But this time, Philip did nothing, and pretended not to see the signals; he did not want one of the best knights in Burgundy to be defeated by a foreigner if he could possibly help it. That would be a terrible humiliation. He expected Lalain to save the situation if there was the slightest chance.

*Below* Lalain is signalling to the Duke to stop the fight, but the Duke pretends not to notice.

# Brave men and referees

The Burgundian Lalain, although at a great disadvantage, struggled on and at last managed to pull the Welshman off balance; Sir Thomas Key fell and was declared the loser. Now it was his turn to appeal. He claimed that it had not been a true fall. Anyone who has watched wrestling on television will know that a man's shoulders and back must be on the canvas before he has lost a fall. It was much the same in a medieval tournament. Sir Thomas pointed out that he had been able to arch himself so as not to fall entirely flat and that therefore he had not been defeated. It was a good argument, but it was not good enough to convince a home referee in front of a home crowd! Sir Thomas had to accept defeat and, worse still, to present his opponent with a fine ruby and a fully-equipped horse.

If the competitors in a joust were so evenly matched that neither of them could score an outright victory, the wise judge would usually declare a draw, with honours even. But men were still unwilling to leave the arena – the first man to go might be thought to have given up. This happened in a foot combat between the French Lord of Charny and a Basque knight called Saavedra. When the judge stopped the fight and declared a draw, the men backed slowly away from each other, axes at the ready, and then halted. There was a long pause; each was determined to uphold his honour and not seem to retreat in front of the other. Then at last the Basque withdrew, leaving the arena to Charny. Everyone was satisfied. It had been the Frenchman who had been "defending the pass", so he had the right to hold it to the last. All the rules had been observed and the rule of honour was satisfied too.

Sometimes the contestants were so evenly matched that only God, represented by the angel in the picture, could decide the match. Usually, the judge would then stop the fight and declare a draw.

# 5. Politics and sport

It is hard to tell whether this battle is part of a tournament or a real war.

The battles in a tournament were so similar to those on a battlefield that it was sometimes hard to tell the two apart. Chroniclers often described wars as if they were tournaments. Sir John Froissart, in his history of the Hundred Years' War between England and France (1338–1453), describes the deeds of prowess by knights on both sides. He was writing for men who loved every detail of a fight and who, when they were not at war, were jousting. During lulls in the war, English and French noblemen often met as friends; they even organized jousts on the battlefield when they got bored with a truce agreed between their leaders.

Edward III started the fashion for founding orders of knights with his Order of the Garter, and many other rulers followed because they saw that these orders could be used for political ends. Duke Philip the Good of Burgundy was one of the greatest rulers in Europe in the fifteenth century, and he founded the Order of the Golden Fleece. He realized that ideals of knightly chivalry could be used to bind his noblemen to the Crown.

For many noblemen, the tournament was the most important thing in life. It kept them busy, and stopped them meddling in politics and intrigue. As one chronicler said: "While the duke jousted with his noblemen, the chancellor and the chamberlain were getting on with the affairs of state".

# Games of war

In a medieval war, much time was spent besieging towns and castles. During a siege, the knights often had to wait for days on end until a breach was made in the walls, and they could lead the attack. So, to amuse themselves, they would in the meantime challenge the knights on the other side to a tournament. Barriers were built out from one of the gates of the town; inside was a party of defenders, outside a party from the attacking army. In this way, the knights could enjoy a good joust without either side winning a military advantage.

Talking about the siege of Neuss in the 1470's, one observer commented: "I don't think there has been such a magnificent siege for more than a hundred years. There were so many knightly combats that it became a school of honour in which to learn the art of war." Young knights without any interest at all in the war would journey from miles around to visit a siege – it was such a marvellous opportunity to learn the arts of chivalry.

The confusion between war and tournament could work the other way too. In 1408, a tournament outside Valencia in Spain looked more like a private war to many of the onlookers. Five knights under the Seneschal of Hainault were pitted against five led by Tollemache of Sainte Coulonne. The two leaders were old enemies; everyone in the crowd knew that they were planning a battle to the death in their so-called tournament, but there was no honourable reason for stopping it. However, King Martin V of Aragon appointed himself President of the proceedings and posted forty armed stewards inside the arena to control things.

The contest had barely started when one of the Seneschal's knights threw down his axe and, with a mighty heave, lifted his enemy into the air; he then pulled out his dagger and got ready to stab him in the

During a siege, the knights from opposing sides would often meet, and even arrange tournaments together.

exposed part of his armour under the armpit. Nobody could argue then when the King moved in to stop what was obviously soon going to be nothing but a brawl.

# The great Dukes of Burgundy

During the fifteenth century the court of the Dukes of Burgundy was one of the most chivalrous in Europe. They ruled a large area of France, which is famous for its wine (and is still known as Burgundy), and also many rich cities in what is now Belgium and Holland. They were the richest and most powerful rulers in Europe, but they were only dukes and were in theory the subjects of the King of France. For many years they struggled to become kings themselves.

The greatest of the Dukes of Burgundy was Philip, called the Good, who reigned from 1419 to 1467. He wanted to build up the most magnificent court in the world. The trade of great towns like Bruges and Ghent made his state very rich, and he also had many fine musicians and painters at his court. When he held a joust, the pennants and display shields were often painted by the great Flemish artist, Jan van Eyck. The court, however, had to obey strict rules of etiquette; the rich feasting and entertainments were usually only held for some very good reason.

For example, in 1454, the year after the great Christian city of Constantinople had fallen to the Turks, the Duke wanted to seem like the champion of Christianity, and impress all Europe with his vow to go on Crusade. So he started the year with a great series of feasts, each one more magnificent than the last. At the height of the most splendid of them all, the Feast of the Pheasant, the Duke suddenly announced in front of the assembled company that he and his noblemen would go on Crusade if the King of France would lead the way.

The magnificent court of the Dukes of Burgundy was famous throughout Europe in the fifteenth century.

The jousting, feasting and entertainments had been going on for days before the Duke made his solemn vow, but it was a great publicity stunt. After months of preparation and excitement, all the nobles in Christendom now knew that the Duke of Burgundy wanted a Crusade and was only held back by his overlord the King of France.

Medieval noblemen used sometimes to settle their differences by meeting in single combat. Here, the Dukes of Brittany and Bourbon are jousting together.

# The politics of sport

In all this state propaganda, jousting had its place too. Duke Philip of Burgundy was recognized as a great expert in all matters of chivalry. Even when he was at war, he would still find time to attend any tournament in the neighbourhood. He knew that he would always receive the place of honour.

On one occasion he used the joust in a very direct way for a political purpose. There was a long-drawn-out dispute between him and the Duke of Saxony about who had the right to the Duchy of Luxembourg; neither side wanted to wage war but neither would give up its claim. So the Duke suggested that he and the Duke of Saxony should meet to settle the issue in single combat. It was a very chivalrous suggestion, but it was not, unfortunately, a very sensible one; the ministers of Saxony pointed out that their Duke was still only a boy – however brave he might be, he would not stand much chance against the most honoured jouster in Europe.

Philip pretended that he had not realized his rival was so young, but said he would instead be willing to fight any other noble member of the court of Saxony. This was the kind of gesture that would impress his followers and, if the challenge were not accepted, public opinion might possibly turn against the Duke of Saxony. In fact, however, Saxony was not willing to risk important claims in the luck of the tournament ring, and the issue remained unresolved.

The most important result of the Duke's love of chivalry was the Order of the Golden Fleece, which he founded in 1430. It was modelled very closely on the Order of Garter, and had a political purpose too. The Duke hoped it would bind together the different nationalities of his nobles, and give them all a sense of unity.

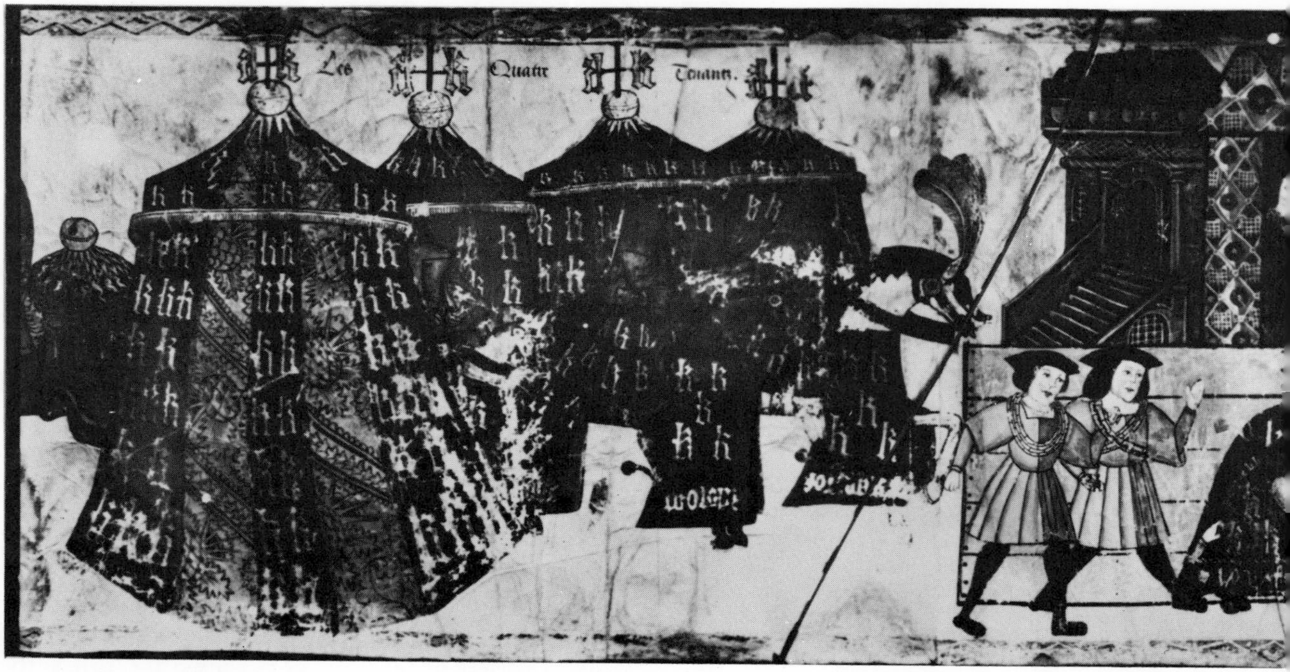

A knight entering the lists.

# Chivalry and prestige

Duke Philip of Burgundy used the world of chivalry to increase his influence. Another French nobleman, René of Anjou, who was much less powerful, devoted what influence he had to keeping the ideals of chivalry alive. For a time René enjoyed the title of King through his family's claim to the kingdom of Naples in Italy. But he had to surrender this title and later he even had to give up his estates around Angers on the Loire. However, "Good King René" is still remembered today, for he left behind an important and interesting book on the subject of tournaments called *The Book of the Tourney*. In it he gives detailed descriptions of the tournaments that were held at his court.

He tells how the lists should be about 160 feet by 200 feet and be surrounded by a strong fence about six feet high fitted with gates. Outside this there should be

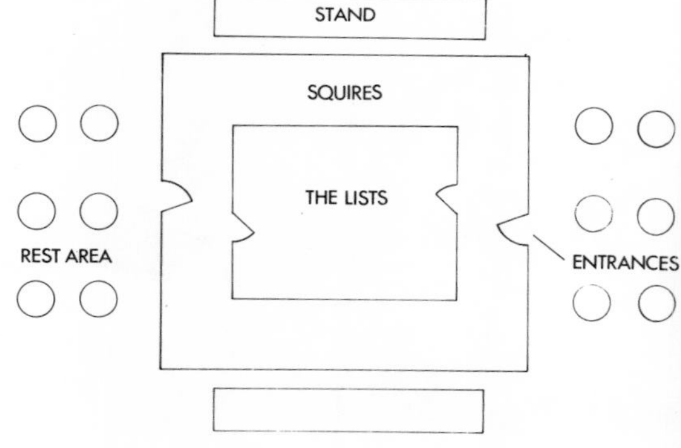


*Above* Plan of a tournament park. *Right* The knights are lined up, waiting for the signal to go. The tournament starts when the axeman cuts the rope.

another fence some twelve feet high, and the space between them was designed to be used as a rest area by competitors and their squires. Behind the twelve-foot fence rose the stands and boxes for the judges and spectators, with special arrangements for the ladies.

At a tournament involving two teams, they were held apart by ropes stretched across the arena. This happened at other tournaments where the rope was cut by the judge. At René's tournaments, however, these ropes were cut by "knights of honour." Once the ropes had been cut, the action started. With a cry of "Laissez aller", which means quite literally "Let's go", the knights charged at one another.

King René was not rich enough to give tournaments as magnificent as those at the court of Burgundy but his reputation among the nobility of France was very high because of his expert knowledge of everything connected with the joust. Thanks to the tournament, a King without a country could still earn fame as a warrior.

# Chivalry in England

In England the tournament was, like most things, far more under the control of the king than on the continent. Even a weak king like Henry III (1216–72) was able to stop quite a number of tournaments from taking place. His son, the great Edward I (1272–1367) made even more restrictions and, while he still held occasional tournaments himself, very few of his barons did so without his express permission. Not that English barons were always peaceful and obedient. Far from it. But they were usually struggling for a say in the Royal Council, rather than trying to set up separate courts of their own.

Yet it was in England that one of the most dangerous political jousts ever was almost staged. This was in 1397, during the reign of Richard II, and was the result of a dispute between Henry, Duke of Hereford and a cousin of the King, and Thomas Mowbray, Duke of Norfolk. Henry who, two years later, was to seize the crown and become King Henry IV, claimed that Norfolk had suggested he was a traitor. He insisted on his right to clear his reputation of the suspicion of treason.

It was arranged that the two dukes would meet at Coventry in October and settle the issue in a trial by battle. If Norfolk won, the words of treason would appear true; if Hereford won, his great power would be further increased. Either way the King would lose influence. And so he stopped the fight.

Henry V, too, was loyal to the code of chivalry. One night, during the great march through France that ended in the victory of Agincourt in 1415, Henry and the advance guard of the army overshot the arranged camp by a few miles. When he realized what had happened, the King did not go back to the camp, but ordered the soldiers to pitch their tents just where they

Henry V ordering his troops to stop for the night.

were – strictly speaking, he was marching against the enemy, and to go back would look like a retreat. The ideals of chivalry were more important to King Henry V than a comfortable night's rest in the safety of the main camp.

# 6. Kings and citizens

The last great days of the tournament were in the fifteenth century. It continued for more than a hundred years after that, but was always then the background to something more important. The new style of warfare had long ago reduced the importance of the knight on the battlefield, and the rise of merchants and bankers was making him less important in society as well.

During the sixteenth century, Europe was troubled by terrible wars between Catholics and Protestants. At the end of them, the medieval idea of a single united Christendom was dead. Instead, men were divided very fiercely over questions of religion. Not even the noble ideals of chivalry that had once been shared by knights everywhere could hold them together any longer.

All that was left then were the great spectacles and shows that had grown up around the tournaments. The tournament became a toy for kings to play with, and even ordinary citizens sometimes took part. It was certainly the most exciting spectator sport Europe would know until grand prix motor racing in the twentieth century.

Tournaments became spectacles for the ordinary citizens to watch, and even take part in.

# Jousting in the town square

Usually, a tournament was held in a temporary stadium set up in the fields outside some town; when it was taken down after the meeting, the materials went to the king-at-arms in charge of the proceedings. Selling the strong wooden beams and brightly coloured linen or satin streamers that had been used to decorate the stands could bring in a lot of money.

Sometimes, however, the nobles would take over a town square. When king Charles VI of France was married in 1389, his new Queen was welcomed into Paris with a tournament which was held in the centre of the city. It was summertime, and the dust rose in clouds as the horses pounded over the untarred streets and squares; two hundred water carriers were specially brought in to try and lay the dust, but they made little difference, and the last jousts had to be held actually in the hall where the wedding banquet was to take place.

An event like this would stop all normal business dealings in the centre of the city, but it brought plenty of trade to the shop-keepers. The windows overlooking the market place made excellent vantage points, and were rented out to spectators; children would climb on to the roofs to get a good view, and the townspeople crowding right up to the barriers often had to be held back by men-at-arms.

To celebrate his marriage to Jane Shore in 1466, King Edward IV held one of the rare English tournaments in the fields of Smithfield, just outside London. Special stands were put up for the rich merchants, and the crowd got the best view they could from ground level; young and adventurous spectators climbed the trees that surrounded the arena. After the jousting was over, people collected the shattered lances as souvenirs.

Sometimes, particularly in Germany, townspeople would hold their own joust in imitation of the nobility,

A tournament in a town square brought the whole city to a standstill.

but this idea did not last long. The sport was much too expensive and time consuming for serious businessmen, even if they did enjoy playing at being knights. As for the knights themselves, they were furious that ordinary citizens should dare to imitate them.

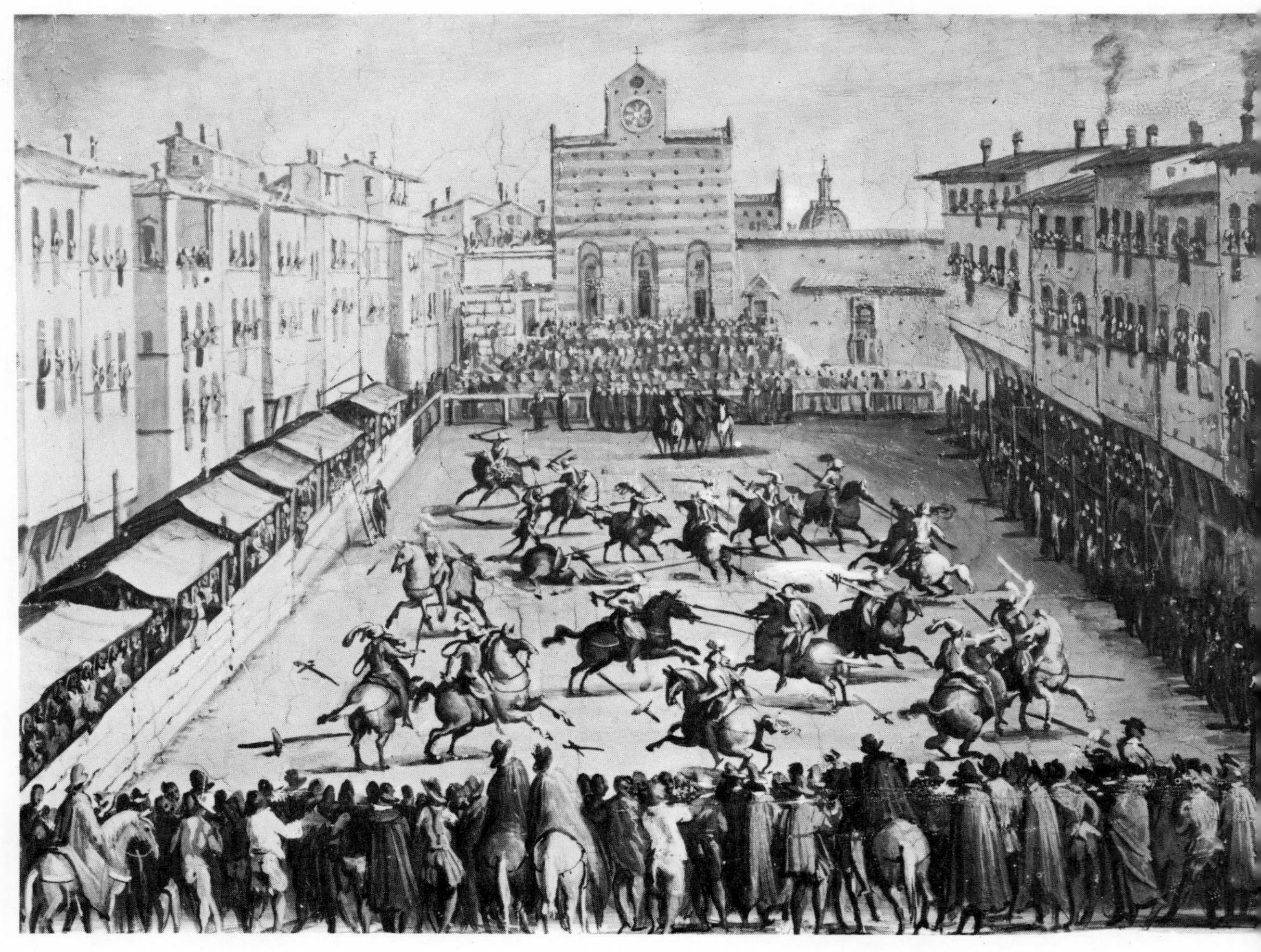

An Italian tournament. It was probably very different from the ones in northern Europe.

## The tournament in Italy

The tournament began in northern Europe, and it did not catch on in the south until much later. In the fifteenth century, however, quite a few tournaments were held in Italy; at first even town officials and citizens took part, but soon it became the preserve of noblemen.

Jousting in Italy was a blending of old and new

styles. It was in Italy that men were beginning to take a new look at the literature of ancient Rome and Greece. We call this movement the Renaissance or "rebirth", and it began with Italian thinkers who had no interest in the strange legends of King Arthur, which they considered a myth from the foggy past of northern Europe. Instead they were trying to bring back to life the glorious past of the Mediterranean peoples, the Greeks and the Romans.

For hundreds of years, the civilization of Europe had been dominated by the northern races. Both the Gothic style of architecture and the tournament had been part of this. But when the tournament reached Italy, it became embroidered with the stories of ancient Greece and Rome, or with other legends that had nothing to do with King Arthur.

Between 1460 and 1480, more than a dozen jousts were held in Florence alone by enthusiastic noblemen. One of them was given by the young Lorenzo dei Medici in 1469, just after he had won recognition as the city's leading citizen. He explains: "To do as others had done, I held a joust in the Piazza of Santa Croce at great expense and with great pomp. I find that we spent about ten thousand ducats."

He was only twenty at the time and he was determined to do the right thing so that his family's great position in the town would not be weakened. Since the Medicis were the strongest family in the town, and since Lorenzo was giving the joust, it is perhaps not surprising that he won a prize, even though he was "not very highly versed in the use of weapons."

# The end of an age

During the sixteenth century, jousting continued in various forms in northern Europe. Some of the most sumptuous tournaments were held at the beginning of the century at the court of the German Emperor Maximilian. He had married Mary, Duchess of Burgundy and heiress of the great Burgundy dukes, so it is not surprising that he should have been interested in the tournament. He invented many different forms of combat, and even introduced some mechanical devices. These included a shield with a section on it that

The Field of the Cloth of Gold was a great display of courtly pageantry by King Henry VIII of England and Francis I of France.

would spring open if the lance hit the right spot. Maximilian's armourers produced some of the most splendid examples of jousting armour that have ever been made.

Across the sea in England, the tournament entered a vivid new era when the handsome and sporting King Henry VIII came to the throne in 1509. His father had left a rich treasury and the young King was determined to have a good time. Scoring sheets that survive show that he was quite good at the sport; he certainly spent money on it – about £4,000 on a single tournament.

In everything he did as a young man, Henry VIII felt himself to be competing with King Francis I of France. They were about the same age; both were considered handsome and both were keen jousters. In 1515, they met outside Calais for a great festival, which they hoped would be the beginning of a long friendship based on the principles of chivalry. It was remembered for years afterwards as the most magnificent event in Europe, and was called the Field of the Cloth of Gold. Unfortunately, many of the events were rained off! But the preparations were tremendous – three thousand lances alone were provided for those taking part.

After Henry VIII, tournaments in England were revived under his daughter, Elizabeth I. Each year a great festival was held to celebrate the day of her accession. These magnificent shows even continued into the reign of the next monarch, James I. The last jousts were held in England in the year 1621. They were to be the last in England for a long, long time.

A trial by battle was a common occurrence in the Middle Ages, and could lead to gruesome scenes.

# Citizen combats

The tournament was the all-action sport of the medieval aristocrat. It was surrounded by noble ideals and colourful legend, and fitted in well with the passion for war that was shared by most noblemen. On the battlefield, fighting and killing were just as brutal as they are today; but in the charmed arena of the tournament, surrounded by pageantry and governed by the book of rules, violence became almost respectable.

Ordinary people were not expected to imitate this lordly pastime. When citizens did stage public fights, as in a trial by battle for example, it was usually very different from the joust. One chronicler describes a trial by battle between two citizens of Ghent. The two men were only wearing short breeches; their heads were completely shaved and their bodies greased all over with fat so that neither could get an unfair grip. The wrestle in the dusty square ended with one of the men being killed and the "trial" was over.

The details of the fight are really nasty; yet sitting in the places of honour above the milling crowd were the same lords and ladies who usually attended tournaments, enjoying every moment of this horrible display. It would seem as though beneath all the pageantry of chivalry lay a far from noble love of violence.

Fighting, however, needs courage, and medieval chroniclers recognized bravery even among peasants when they saw it on the battlefield. One chronicler described: "A little peasant man of humble status, who was so valiant that day that, if he had been of gentle blood so that I could record his name, I should have testified with all honour to him. For true valour should be applauded in the low as well as the high."

Today, the sport of jousting is being revived with great success, and a group of men are trying to make it a recognized sport once again. At the moment there are noblemen amongst them; indeed, to the medieval kings and dukes in this book, they would seem mere "little peasant men of humble status." But these modern sportsmen are men of "true valour" and we can be sure that, although they are not of "gentle blood" their names will soon be recorded, if only in the record books.

This joust at the court of the French King Louis XIV in 1662 is a very colourful affair, but bears little relation to the tournaments of the Middle Ages.

# Table of dates

| | |
|---|---|
| 450–500 | Period during which the historical figure of King Arthur is supposed to have lived. |
| 1062 | Death of Godfrey of Preuilly. He was the first man to draw up a set of rules for the tournament. |
| 1066 | William the Conqueror invades England. |
| 1096 | The Crusades begin. |
| 1130 | Pope Innocent II bans all tournaments. |
| *c* 1136 | Geoffrey of Monmouth publishes his book, *A History of the Kings of Britain*, which tells the stories of King Arthur. |
| 1156 | The first Crusader joust held at Antioch. |
| 1167 | William Marshall is dubbed knight and enters his first tournament. |
| 1179 | Coronation of Philip II of France – more than a thousand knights celebrate by jousting. |
| 1219 | William Marshall dies, aged about 73. |
| 1223 | The first Round Table tournament is held in Cyprus. |
| 1227 | Ulrich of Lichtenstein sets out as a knight errant and is a great success. |
| 1267 | King Edward I issues a Statute of Arms to stop the rioting that accompanied tournaments. |
| 1299 | Edward I holds an Arthurian feast to celebrate his marriage to Margaret of France. |
| 1316 | Pope John XXII lifts the Church's ban on tournaments. |
| 1344 | A Round Table tournament at Windsor Castle, which gives Edward III the idea for the Order of the Garter. |
| 1346 | Battle of Crécy: English archers defeat the French cavalry. |
| 1349 | First formal meeting of the Order of the Garter. |

| | |
|---|---|
| 1389 | Wedding of the French King Charles VI is celebrated by a great tournament in the centre of Paris. |
| 1398 | A joust between the dukes of Norfolk and Hereford is stopped at the last moment by King Richard II. |
| 1408 | A violent tournament outside Valencia is stopped by King Martin V of Aragon. |
| 1415 | The Battle of Agincourt. |
| 1430 | Duke Philip of Burgundy founds the Order of the Golden Fleece. |
| 1443 | *Pas d'armes* or passage of arms of the Tree of Charlemagne. |
| 1453 | Constantinople captured by the Turks. |
| 1454 | The Feast of the Pheasant at the court of Burgundy, where the tournament is used for political purposes. |
| 1466 | Jousts held at Smithfield, London, to celebrate the wedding of Edward IV to Jane Shore. |
| 1469 | Lorenzo dei Medici holds a magnificent tournament in Florence. |
| 1475 | Siege of Neuss, to which many knights travelled to learn the arts of chivalry. |
| 1515 | The Field of the Cloth of Gold; a tournament of goodwill held by Henry VIII of England and Francis I of France. |
| 1621 | The last tournament in England before the modern revival is held during the reign of James II. |

# Glossary

ACHIEVEMENT The full armorial bearings of a family, including the shield, the helmet, the crest, the mantling and the motto.

A OUTRANCE Applied to weapons that have not been specially blunted for the joust.

CHARGE The designs that make up a coat of arms.

COAT OF ARMS Originally just the armorial shield, although now loosely used to mean the same as "achievement".

CORONAL The point of a jousting lance that has been blunted by being splayed and then bound up.

DESTRIER A heavy warhorse.

TO DUB To make somebody a knight, by touching their shoulders with a sword.

ENTREPRENEUR A French word meaning someone who takes things in hand; used to describe the organizer of a tournament.

FABULATORES Latin name for the wandering bards who spread the stories of King Arthur.

HERALDS Officials who carried messages in war, and later dealt with coats of arms and all matters of chivalry.

JOUST An organized combat between two men on horseback.

KING AT ARMS A senior herald who helped arrange a tournament.

KNIGHT A man, usually of noble birth, who has taken vows to protect the weak and uphold the honour of chivalry.

KNIGHT ERRANT A wandering knight, touring in search of adventure.

LISTS The barriers surrounding the arena for a formal joust. Hence men "entered the lists."

MANTLING The flowing trappings that covered a jouster's horse. In heraldry, the term applies to the draperies that surround a coat of arms.

PAS D'ARMES, OF PASSAGE OF ARMS An elaborate form of

tournament in which the organizers pretended to hold a difficult mountain pass.

PENNON A short pointed banner at the end of a lance.

PIKE An infantry weapon consisting of a long wooden shaft armed with a sharp blade.

PALFREY A light horse for travelling.

QUINTAIN A training target for jousters.

REBATED WEAPONS Weapons that have been blunted or treated in some way to make them less dangerous.

REFUGE The enclosure at a tournament in which knights rested or received first aid.

ROLL OF ARMS A catalogue listing all the noble families and the coats of arms they claimed the right to use.

ROUNCEY A second-rate horse, a hack.

ROUNDEL A round plate, usually rising to a point in the centre, which was strapped on to protect the joints in a suit of armour.

SQUIRE A young man learning to be a knight, who helped a knight with his armour and horses.

SUMPTER A slow heavy horse for carrying baggage.

TROUBADOUR A medieval poet or story teller, usually from Provence in the south of France.

TOURNEY, or TOURNAMENT A contest between two parties of armed men on horseback.

VAMPLACE A round plate that flared out at the base of a lance to protect the hand.

VIGIL An all-night watch kept in church by a young man before he was made knight.

VIZOR The hinged face-guard on a helmet.

# Further Reading


Richard Barber, *The Knight and Chivalry* (Longman, 1970)

Kenneth Fowler, *The Age of Plantagenet and Valois* (Elek, 1967)

Jean Froissart, *Chronicles*, selected and translated by Geoffrey Brereton (Penguin, 1968)

Geoffrey of Monmouth, *The History of the Kings of Britain*, translated by Lewis Thorpe (Penguin, 1966)

Geoffrey Hindley, *The Medieval Establishment* (Wayland, 1970)

Geoffrey Hindley, *Medieval Warfare* (Wayland, 1971)

Geoffrey Hindley, *Castles of Europe* (Hamlyn, 1968)

Maurice Keen, *The Laws of War in the Late Middle Ages* (Routledge & Kegan Paul, 1965)

R. R. Sellman, *Mediaeval English Warfare* (Methuen, 1960)

R. W. Southern, *The Making of the Middle Ages* (Hutchinson, 1967)

Henry Treece and Ewart Oakeshott, *Fighting Men* (Brockhampton Press, 1963)

Frederick Wilkinson, *Arms and Armour* (Hamlyn, 1971)

# Index

# Picture Credits

The Publishers wish to thank the following for their kind permission to reproduce copyright illustrations on the pages mentioned: the Trustees of the British Museum, *jacket* (front, back and flaps), 8, 10, 11, 28, 37, 38–39, 43, 44–45, 47, 48, 53, 64, 68, 71; the Radio Times Hulton Picture Library, *frontispiece*, 9, 13, 16, 17, 20, 23, 24–25, 29, 30–31, 34, 35, 41, 72, 74–75, 79, 82–83, 86–87; the Mansell Collection, 14–15, 25 (top), 26–27, 33, 56–57, 58–59, 76–77 (top), 80, 84, 89; the Trustees of the Wallace Collection, 42. Other illustrations appearing in this book are the property of the Wayland Picture Library.

Drawings by John Walters.